VIOLENCE

THALEN VALE

To my mother: I am forever grateful for the peace and shelter you've provided me throughout my life. I am always reminded that the world is dangerous, but I can always come home to you.

CONTENTS

PREFACE

This collection isn't one about
war, politics, crime, or trauma.

It is about violence that precedes and succeeds it.

Violence is not an act fixed in time,
but a force that persists across it,
beyond what is seen,
beyond what is done.

Not the moment of harm,
but what remains undone.

It predates us.
It will outlast us.

ACT I - INVOCATION OF FORCE

MEMENTO MORI

*Petals fall
into a nameless valley,
slowly,
each one stained
crimson.*

*Thunder echoes
between the valley walls,
deafening,
though none remain
to hear it,
as the petals break.*

*The sky erupts,
weeping countless tears
onto the parched earth,
pressing the shattered petals
into the soil.*

Memento mori.

PRIMORDIAL

Space tears itself open,
ripping into darkness,
expanding beyond measure.

Stars burn brighter,
phosphorescent and indifferent,
like a ballerina performing for no one,
departing the stage without a glance,
detonating in glorious farewell.

Planets form unseen,
birth children of their own,
age without witness,
collapse without care,
become belts of drifting stone,
their children none the wiser.

Debris collides,
scatters,
pelts whatever drifts into its path,
indiscriminately.

Violence requires no one.
It is primordial.

GARDENER

Across every world that holds an atmosphere,
the work continues.

Land is moved, oceans raised,
mountains worn to plains,
soil turned for what grows next,
warmth given to some,
cold to others.

It does not consider the cost.
It only continues.

What some call a violent storm
irrigates the soil.
What some call a devastating quake
is only a farmer
tilling its land.

GUARD AGAINST THE UNSEEN

A blade cannot kill
without a hand to guide it.

The force behind the strike
is the weight of intent.

Guard not against the foe before you,
but against what rises within.

Stay vigilant at dusk,
when enemies are unseen,
not those revealed
by dawn's light.

The greatest threat to this watch
is the one you know best,
yet never see.

PARRICIDE

Yes, you birthed me,
raised and scolded me,
but this blood is not a leash,
nor a debt I owe in silence.

I am my own being,
free to live and breathe
however I dare.

So I shed your golden blood,
that which you were so proud of,
sever the tie between us,
dying my own blood red,
and walk this world alone.

*Your shadow may trail me
however far you reach,
but I will not turn back
to answer your cry.*

*May I be the first,
oh,
Glorious Parricide.*

ACT II - DESECRATION

ANNIHILATION

Desolate wastes. Trembling soil.

Bleached bones beneath ashen earth,
how long has it been?

Crimson tides, crashing waves;
blood spilled into violent seas,
how long—has—it—been?

Barren sky. Screaming wind.

Scattered souls adrift on air,
how long—must—it—go—on?

Burning bodies. Raging flame.

Viscera swallowed in the fire,
how long—before—it—ends?

Where are you?

Where are we?

Annihilation.

MUSEUM OF EXISTENCE

Gallery I: A Diorama of Storms—
winds corked in glass,
a jar of floods,
lightning preserved in crystal.

Gallery II: An Exhibit of Violence—
a blade rusted with memory,
rope stiffened by breath,
powder that still hungers for flame.

Gallery III: Stained Glass of the Cosmos—
a supernova's burst,
a black hole's mouth,
an imploding sky.

Gallery IV: Archives of Devotion—
altars toppled into dust,
icons eroded by tears,
a prayer sealed in amber.

Gallery V: Relics of Civilization—
coins corroded with salt,
books burned to ghost-script,
a clock whose hands no longer move.

Gallery VI: Chamber of Silence—
tongues pressed in wax,
a bell without a clapper,
the echo of a vanished choir.

Our galleries offer only the finest remnants,
carefully gathered,
patiently displayed.

The world entrusted to us
has been kept.

LINGUICIDE

Countless years of effort,
sound becoming meaning,
emotion made transmittable,
stories carried on the tongue,
culture passed mouth to mouth.

Then in a hundred years or less,
others arrive and write over yours,
their words displacing your own,
their conquests replacing your stories,
their silence swallowing your songs.

What is a language
but a memory of sound
fading into time,
or broken by a stronger fist.

Language lost in the silence of others.

ECOCIDE

Millions of years spent
giving birth and raising
a host of beautiful creations:
tall trees rooted in ancient soil,
flowers that perfumed the wind,
animals tuned to every season,
and last, her most proud creation:
the human.

Yet the ones she was most proud of
took half that time
to exploit her flesh,
poison her blood,
choke her air,
and leave her a husk.

The efforts of a mother
spoiled by her children.

SOCIAL CONTRACT

I offered a portion of freedom
for protection within your borders.
At first, the cost was small.

My son may be drafted for war
but that is patriotism.

Then you took a portion of my salary
and offered services in exchange.

Now my sons are sent for resources,
the services grow fewer.

A child was killed in a place of learning.
A neighbor fell to a bullet with no name on it.
Another grows sick in a waiting room
they cannot afford to leave.

Where is the contract I signed?
Was this in the agreement?

They grind us down,
these institutions,
rendering citizens
into product.

LOVELESS

Your silence,
a sear
burned into my soul.

Your words,
thorns
driving deeper
into flesh.

Your presence,
a wraith
I have learned
to avoid.

You led me
into false trust,
one I held dearly,
leading me further astray,
losing everything
that was truly real.

ACT III - CONSUMMATION

APEX

Lost in a paradise of blood
it boils within,
crimson steam spreading throughout.

A hunger suppressed
can never be sated.

Steel through flesh and bone,
an unending horde
seeks to end this slaughter.

But the feast must continue,
else the devourer becomes
the devoured.

Sharpen the instinct.
Trust the hunger.
Consume or be consumed.

Do not relent.
Become the Apex.

MASTERPIECE

Use my blood
as your paint.

Scatter me
like starlight
across this
pitch-black canvas.

Stab the board
a bloom erupting
like a chrysanthemum.

Strike across
with the fury of
Zeus.

Wash it clean
in the tears
I can no longer shed.

*Dust it
with the ashes
of my ground bones.*

*Make a masterpiece
from my suffering.*

STRIKE IT

Ah, ooo!
Strike it!

Incendiary,
Inflammatory.

Ah, yeah!
Strike it!

Put us to the torch,
burn this,
house of straw.

Ooo, ah!
Strike it!

Let the heat swell,
let the flame burst.

Yeah, like that.
Strike it!

Consume us,
blazing away.

AWAKENING

Crimson carnations weep,
sanguine tears that seep
into the ground they keep.

The sun scorches above
with a merciless love,
its rays torch the earth below.

Scarlet skies shudder,
split asunder,
withered soil torn open.

Something stirs beneath.
The land trembles.

What rises has no name for mercy.

DEATH IS ART

Ah—ah!
Plunge it
through my chest,
let the colors burst.

Mm—mm!
A bullet rolls
across my palm,
bang, canvas complete.

Ha—ha!
Strike the match,
watch it bloom,
light devours light.

Ah. Ha. Mm. Ah.
Hang me in the gallery,
still trembling,
beauty,
immortalized.

SUFFERING

Birthed like porcelain,
fragile, unmarked.

It starts with a tumble,
then the collapse
of a tower of blocks.

Proceeds with the cruelty
of other children,
thoughtless words,
careless hands.

Followed by the heartbeat
one gives to another,
then the arrest
that shortly follows.

Then the fracture
in a house once united,
an ice age settling
over rooms once warm.

Adulthood arrives like a bill:
education that costs you years,
labor that costs you more,
credit deciding your horizon.

Then the body turns:
you ran once,
now the stairs require negotiation.
What carried you effortlessly
now asks for permission.

And none of this accounts
for those who carry
an additional weight,
skin judged before it is known,
a mind measured by the wrong ruler,
a love condemned before it is lived.

Life's tribulations accumulate,
until they don't.

A bruised skeleton laid into the ground.
A worn soul returning to where it began.

ACT IV - AFTERMATH

LAUGHING WITH THE REAPER

He arrives wearing
a weathered leather coat,
brim wide,
shadow deep.

A gentleman of middling years,
cane in one hand,
pocket watch in the other.

He's seen it all:
the one who stopped the bus,
the one who couldn't swim,
the one who tried peanuts,
the one who flew without wings,
the one who forgot his fear of heights.

Each story earns
a quiet chuckle,
a laugh to break
the stillness of the air.

And when he turns to me,
I laugh with him.

WRATH

I fucking hate you.

A year of silence. A year of strain.
The thread snapped and the world recoiled.

You loved the lights.
The terrace crowned you in neon.
Clubs where hands found you.
You drank until your mouth forgot mercy.
You slept on borrowed couches and called it
safety.

You cheated.
You lied. Again and again.
You left crumbs of feeling,
enough to keep me starving.
You lied as easily as breathing.
You warmed me like a stage prop,
then coldly rehearsed your absence.
Your apologies were coins dropped into
a well you never planned to climb from.

Would your mother be proud
of the hollow you parade?
Do your friends love you,
or the pretty photograph you sell them?
Do the men who touch you
ever look at the ruin beneath your hands?

You treated danger like traffic,
ordinary, survivable.
Powders, bottles, strangers,
thrills you called harmless.
You carried that rot home.
You spread it under my door.

Keep your lights.
Keep your crowd.
Keep the applause.
Wear their praise like tinfoil, shiny, thin,
ready to tear.

When the lights die, there will be echoes.
When the mask falls, there will be silence.
When the room empties, nothing but your
name will remain, and it will be small.

You already killed what I gave you.
My love is molten now,
corrosive,
radioactive grief.
It glows. It remembers. It burns like testimony.

Step into the noise and let it swallow you.
Drown in the echo of your own applause.
Be forgotten by the crowd you begged to see you.
Let the river take your reflection
and give nothing back.

The anger cools into metal.
It hardens into an indictment I can carry.
I will not forgive you. I will keep this verdict.

I am furious.
I am wounded.
I am still human.

SURVIVOR

This world is boundlessly cruel,
leaving us destitute,
empty.

All I had has been taken,
I raised no fist,
had no force behind it.

The flowers have gone grey,
the people faceless,
the sky perpetually overcast.
It feels like dusk
even when I wake.

I find work among the unscrupulous,
disposing of what remains
after punishment is dealt
to blameless victims
who could have been me,
and taking from those
whose abundance won't miss it.

After a long day,
I inject medicine into my soul
just to see color
for a moment.

I continue.
Not because it is good.
Not because it gets easier.

Only because I am still here,
and that, for now,
is enough.

DNA

My father, his father, and their father
before them,
an ancestry with a single tradition:
exploit others before they could exploit us.
Were we ever truly threatened?
Was such a plan in motion?
Unknown.

We were born with a knife in hand
and graduated with a gun.

Steel and gunpowder expended,
families broken,
tears enough to form a river,
blood enough to fill an ocean.

Our wives are chosen from the daughters
of families we destroyed,
raised to forget what was taken,
to serve one purpose:
continuing the line.

A tradition of violence.
A culture of death.
An inheritance of blood.

A day may come when it is severed,
but that day will not end violence.

ACT V - WITNESS

JOURNALISM

My career began
with small town specials:
festivals, contests,
ribbon cuttings.

The content grew boring.
I wanted more.

Not gunfire,
something safer, I told myself.
The first scene was sad
but digestible.
Trees seem to attract drunks.

The second, difficult,
still manageable.
Gang colors.
Unregistered guns.
Teens who never made graduation.
The third.

I arrived at a house
my salary could never afford,
opulent, castle-like,
the kind that invites siege
in less civilized times.

We weren't permitted inside.
I saw enough.

Senior officers staggering out,
releasing their stomachs
into the rose bushes.

Forensics entering,
then leaving seconds later,
their job unfinished.

EMS arriving,
firefighters had to hold them up.
No gurneys left that house.
Only bags.
Refuse removal.

A family of six, now none.
The youngest: one month.
The oldest: terminal,
with only months remaining,
though the house decided otherwise.

They discouraged us
from requesting photographs.

I had a job to do.

Until I didn't.

VERDICT

I sit in this hallowed room,
hair greying with every passing case
brought before me.

With every verdict, I feel righteous.
With every verdict, I feel hopeless.

A dog left in a car
on a summer day,
sun at its peak,
the owner inside,
choosing a new cage.

A baby abandoned in a tub,
high tides in a quiet room,
down the corridor, down the stairs,
the mother at the front door
signing for her new crib.

A schoolboy in the street,
chasing a ball into traffic,
the car that took him
already late for a maternity ward,
rushing toward a birth.

For the devious, the cruel, the deliberate:
my gavel does not hesitate.

They know what they did.

But these,
who looked away for a moment,
who chose something small
over something irreplaceable,
I hesitate.

And still,
a verdict is delivered.

BYSTANDER

The digital clock felt frozen,
probably a glitch,
my boss grew angrier by the hour,
my children hungry at home.

I caught one train, then another.
Someone was pushed onto the track
of my final train,
a delay that felt like purgatory,
but my kids were fed.

The wall clock needed a battery.
Our teacher droned on,
back facing the class.
I scrolled through my phone,
the dead filled my feed like weather.

*We almost made it to dismissal
before the PA roared around us.
This was not a drill.*

Hours later, uniforms opened our doors.

*We walked past tiny bodies
and made our way home,
just in time for dinner
and video games.*

DEICIDE

Those who suffer violence
rarely see its full shape,
only the fragment that finds them,
only the weight they can carry.

Sickness. Sin. Starvation.
A child born into destitution.
A body outliving its dignity.
These are the faces closest to us.

But beyond what we can hold,
violence moves without witness,
pure as water,
and just as indifferent
to what it drowns.

We do not weep for the stars
and their final performance.
We do not mourn the motherly planets
who collapsed in silence
long before we arrived.

Our universe will end too,
taking all it ever birthed.
No heavenly body will grieve it.
Something else will take its place.

If there are gods,
they know this.
They have watched long enough
to stop calling it tragedy.

They bow to it,
as all things must.

Even gods die.

Violence endures.

www.ingramcontent.com/pod-product-compliance
Lightning Source LLC
Chambersburg PA
CBHW020508160726

47991CB00007B/2861